Raindrops keep falling on my tent

Joy Mackay

Contents

1. Rain Can Be Beautiful 2
2. All-Camp Activities 3
3. Cabin Activities 9
4. Individual Activities 14

Sources 18

Bibliography 19

Library of Congress Cataloging in Publication Data

Mackay, Joy.
  Raindrops keep falling on my tent.

1. Camp.   2. Indoor games.   3. Amusements.
  I. Title.
  GV198.R4M32   796.54   80-26833

ISBN 0-87603-060-6
Copyright 1981 American Camping Association
Library of Congress

American Camping Association
Martinsville, Indiana

1
Rain Can Be Beautiful

"Is that rain I hear on the roof?" These words can strike terror in the heart of a camp leader. Rain . . . mud puddles . . . soggy bedding . . . wet campers . . . sore throats . . . homesickness . . . a whirl of nightmarish thoughts begin.

Relax! A rainy day in camp can be a delightful experience if you plan for it to be that way.

Check your own attitude first of all. Be positive. "Hooray, it's raining!" Be excited and even enthusiastic about the rain. Maybe it will settle the dust on the camp road or break that muggy hot spell. And probably the farmers need it, so be thankful. And even if it is your sixth straight day of rain and you've planned an ark-building class for your third activity period, accept the challenge to your ingenuity. Attitudes are contagious, and camp spirit should run high regardless of weather.

If your campers have had a full schedule, a more relaxed rainy day schedule may be welcomed by both campers and staff. Arrange with the cooks to have breakfast an hour later if it is pouring rain at daybreak. This usually makes for good sleeping weather, and an extra hour in the morning or extra rest time after lunch may be much appreciated.

If you are enjoying a warm, gentle summer rain, plan to follow your regular camp program as much as possible. Be sure campers are dressed properly if it is chilly. Rain gear, ponchos, and boots prevent sniffles later on. In a warm rain, swimming can be fun. Many campers have never had the opportunity at home to do this. As long as there isn't a thunderstorm and as long as campers do not get chilled, a water party can add excitement to your program. You may want to provide hot chocolate and, to prevent colds, have campers dry briskly and put on dry, warm clothing after a rain swim.

Lifesaving class can have dry land drills on holds, releases, and carries, regardless of weather. And this is a good time to read that textbook in preparation for the written exam.

Your archery class can repair arrows and bows and make new targets on rainy days. Possibly you may have a rain shelter where campers can shoot safely.

The campcraft class really needs a rainy day to test its skills. Anyone can lay a fire and cook on a sunny day, but a good campcrafter can light fires, cook, and stay dry even in a downpour. This is a real test of your camper's abilities. A log can be split for the dry wood in the center. Previously waterproofed matches will be needed. These can be coated with nail polish or paraffin. Lashing a tarp high over your fire site will allow your cooks to prepare and cook food under shelter. If your campers have previously constructed a lean-to or an outpost site, they may choose to spend all day and all night at their own campsite.

A canoeing class can be conducted as usual as long as there is no electrical storm. Your canoeing campers will be in swimsuits anyhow, and it is rather exciting to do things in the rain if dressed for it. At home Johnnie is probably called into the house when it rains, but at camp he can carry on some regular activities even in wet weather.

Musical groups, handcrafts, creative writing, sketching, and drama groups have no problem meeting as usual. The nature class finds the rain helpful for finding salamanders, moss, or spider webs. Put on your rain togs for a puddle hike!

Though you may continue your regular schedule on the first and second days of rain, you'd better introduce some exciting innovations by the third day of the monsoon. Here are points to remember:

1. *Plan in advance for rainy days.* During precamp training with your staff, brainstorm rainy day ideas. Make elaborate preparations for rainy day activities. Develop plans A, B, C, and D for consecutive days of liquid sunshine. Save lots of surprises and special events that will be used only if it rains, and you'll have campers and staff alike hoping for that rainy day.

2. *Check out your camp facilities and personnel for rainy day programming.* What use can be made of the dining hall other than meals? The camp library? The stables? The camp store? The chapel? What talents do your counselors have? Don't forget your noncounseling staff. Your nurse may have a hobby worth sharing. Your cook may teach campers to bake cookies. Your bus driver may know something about forestry.

3. *Keep your plans flexible.* You may have to shift plans several times in one day if a warm rain becomes a northeaster, or the rain clears. Be sensitive to your campers' needs. Each camping period will be different. What was successful during that week of rain in July may not work in August.

4. *Plan with the needs of your individual campers in mind.* Cindy may be bursting with energy while Sherry would rather write letters. Ten-year-old Tom could fish all day, while his 15-year-old brother Jim would rather perfect his hook shot on the basketball court. Keep individual differences in mind as you plan your program, and always remember that the program is only a tool to

accomplish your objectives. In no case should a program become an end in itself, or you will find that you are pushing campers into your program mold, rather than developing a program around campers' needs.

5. *Plan for maximum camper involvement.* Campers learn in proportion to their involvement. (And so do you.) If you want campers to get the most out of their camping period, provide experiences where they can be totally involved. This means you will have some all-camp activities, some cabin group activities, and some individual activities. You might use a rainy day committee made up of representative campers and a few counselors to carry out rainy day programs.

6. *Some activities are best done in the rain.* Save these and provide them only when it rains. Keep the element of surprise in your wet weather program. Juniors especially appreciate this. This doesn't mean no advance planning, but just the opposite. Plan to keep a secret from your campers and announce with great fanfare the "special surprise" in the dining hall or when you have the whole camp together.

You can make a rainy day something to anticipate with pleasure rather than a dull and dreary blight to your camp program.

2
All-Camp Activities

"Is it still raining?" The inflection which accompanies this question is important. If it's asked with weariness, step up your activities. If it's asked with excitement, you're a winner!

How about breakfast in bed? (Are you out of your mind?) If you have a small camp or a large camp with a small counselor-camper ratio, this can be accomplished without much effort, and it won't be a burden on the kitchen staff either. Counselors can carry trays of milk and dry cereal (the kind you can eat right in the box) and a pitcher of hot chocolate. Campers can use their own cups or plastic-coated paper cups. Breakfast is served to campers in bed. What a delightful surprise for a dreary morning! It is a light breakfast, but one campers will long remember.

Or you may sleep in an extra hour on the third day of rain, but be sure to notify the kitchen staff and all of the counselors beforehand. A little extra sleep may greatly improve attitudes and eliminate irritability among campers who need more rest than the average camp program provides. And this may be meeting a very real physical need for your staff. Then when your day does begin be sure it is action-packed. A long-term camp can afford to be more relaxed than a short-term camp. One week campers want action every minute.

* * *

Run a Wells Fargo game in the rain. This is a wild game of the West. Be sure campers are dressed in old clothes. Divide the camp into two teams. A piece of adhesive tape marked with the team color is placed on the forehead of each camper. Teams try to "capture" the mail or treasure and take it to their home base. A team member is considered "scalped" or dead and out of the game when the adhesive tape is pulled from his head. The object is to scalp the enemy team and capture the treasure. It is a rough and wild game. High schoolers particularly enjoy it. In a coed camp, you may want to make a rule that boys attack only boys and girls attack only girls.

* * *

An all-camp treasure hunt can be fun in the rain if campers are dressed for the weather. Treasure can be stones painted with gold paint or some goodies to eat hidden in a metal container.

* * *

A scavenger hunt by cabins or teams can also be successful in the rain and campers will keep warm running over the entire campground. You can have each group find the objects in the order you give them or have each team run for the object as a group. The whole team must go together for each object. Include in your list some things easy to find on a rainy day such as a toad, a

4/Raindrops Keep Falling on My Tent

salamander, or a snail. You may also include such things as a 5" piece of string or a hair from the camp director's chest (if you can find him), or the waterfront director's whistle. (There may be only one.) Include things that campers will have to figure out, such as a picture of Lincoln (penny or stamp or $5 bill), a thermometer registering 100 degrees. They may draw one or heat a real thermometer to that exact temperature. You may include any missing items around camp, such as a counselor's car keys or a lost watch.

* * *

A photography class may enjoy picture-taking in the rain. Close-ups or rain on a puddle or drops of water on a leaf can be beautiful, but you need a good camera for these shots. Campers in this class might spend time learning picture composition or developing prints. Enlargements can be made if the equipment is available or the arts of cropping and vignetting may be tried.

* * *

Moving pictures or slides can be kept on hand for rainy days. Prior to bad weather take candid shots of camp personnel as well as campers for a rainy day surprise showing; or take slides of unusual locations around camp and have campers try to locate where this tree or that gnarled stump is located. A shot of someone's boot or a roof of a building taken at an unusual angle will make it more difficult to recognize.

* * *

Hold an indoor track meet. Both cabin groups and individuals can compete in various events. Involve the whole camp in such events as the discus throw (paper plates), javelin throw (paper straws), shot put (bean bags, pillows, or balloons), long jump, high jump, hop skip and jump, and the indoor mile (50 feet with ankles tied).

* * *

A good change of pace might be to have cabin games on a rainy afternoon. A different game is played in each cabin; campers rotate around to the different cabins every half hour. Include a story cabin. Young campers enjoy this.

* * *

How about an indoor county fair? This takes most of a day to prepare. Each cabin sets up a booth made of chairs, blankets, tables, or anything campers can find. Each cabin has a different display or game of skill. One cabin might have water guns to shoot out a candle flame; another might offer prizes to anyone who can shave a balloon without breaking it (take the blades out of the razors first!). Or put a counselor behind a poncho with just his head sticking out. Have campers throw wet sponges at him. Use campers' imagination and see how original they can be with their booths. Each cabin may enter a prize vegetable, such as a large head of lettuce (basketball wrapped in green paper) or a pie (mud pie). Add an arts and crafts display and a camper dressed as some farm animal for the livestock exhibit. Award ribbons for first, second, and third prizes, honorable mention, best in class. You can include a trained animal show with campers dressed in costumes and going through the antics of these animals.

* * *

Save an all-camp birthday party for a rainy day. Divide campers according to the months of their birthdays. Afternoon hours can be spent decorating your dining room tables with motifs for different months. December could have Christmas decorations, February could use hearts or cherries and hatchets. October's table has Halloween decorations and November's uses turkeys and pilgrims. Campers eat with those who share their birthday month. Each group can supply entertainment related to that season of the year.

* * *

A semiformal dinner with candlelight and music might add just the right touch after running around all day in grubbies. Or your junior high or high schoolers might enjoy a banquet "date" night.

* * *

Try a color day when everyone wears a bright color. One day may be orange and everyone who can wears something with that color in it. Bright colors help lift spirits on a dull day. Try a striped day or a plaid day. One camp had an inside-out day, and clothes were worn at least part of the day inside-out.

* * *

Give campers instruction in the use of map and compass. This is a good indoor activity. You can practice giving bearings and distances and then go on an imaginary trip by using topographical maps and Silva compasses. Designate a starting point, then give campers consecutive readings such as: Go 025 degrees for 2 1/2 miles. Have them mark this on their maps. Then go 190 degrees for 3/4 mile. What do you find there? Or you could give 15 or 20 readings and see how many end at the right place. Later when you have a sunny day, you may want to actually follow the route you laid out on that rainy day.

* * *

Have a counselor-camper day. Campers elect peers to be the director, nurse, waterfront director, etc. In each cabin one camper is elected to be counselor for the day. Be sure your staff realizes that this does not relieve them of responsibility, but only increases it. The director for the day assumes the role by making the announcements, and taking on whatever the director does that day. Nurse for the day assists the real nurse all day. The real counselors play the roles of the campers who are taking their place. This can be fun as campers see the counselors act like campers and vice versa. Beach staff for the day (for a rainy day swim) works with the regular guards.

* * *

If you have an outdoor shelter, try a Paul Bunyan day. Include woodchopping, sawing, naildriving, bedroll making, knapsack packing, and boiling water on a hobo stove. Try log rolling from one marker to another. Choose a log that is larger at one end than the other, so that as it is rolled corrections will have to be made to straighten its course. Each event can be timed to see who finishes in the best time.

* * *

Spend an hour singing favorite camp songs. This can be around the tables after a meal or in a meeting place. Remember that a singing camp is a happy camp, rain or shine. Sing songs appropriate to the age group and pitched for their voices. If an evening meeting must be indoors because of the weather, spend more time singing. If you have an indoor fireplace, singing by firelight will add an impressive atmosphere. Teach *good* music. If you teach appreciation for lovely songs of the outdoors, campers will not miss other music. Select a good leader. He does not have to be a good singer or musician, but he must know how to lead the group and be sensitive to group atmosphere.

* * *

A rainy day is perfect for the camp choir or chorus to practice or prepare for a musical presentation. A camp orchestra or band can prepare special numbers. These musical groups, along with your drama club, can present some worshipful programs.

* * *

Conduct a songwriting contest by cabins. Include the best song in your camp songbook next year.

* * *

What could be better on a rainy day than a camp circus, complete with clowns, elephants, and a parade? Use a meeting place or dining hall for the big top. Decorate with streamers like a huge circus tent. Each cabin can put on a sideshow using sheets and rope for props. One cabin can have the Siamese twins (two small campers in one large sweat shirt), the fat man, the bearded lady, etc. One cabin can be the band with comb hummers and drums made from tin cans. Another cabin may present a wild animal act, another may want to supply the clowns or a tightrope walker (walk along a rope on the floor with appropriate gestures). Two campers under a blanket can become an elephant. A stuffed knee sock makes a trunk. A parade of elephants holding each others' trunks opens the circus. And of course each sideshow has a barker inviting everyone in. Supper can be part of the circus with hot dogs, potato chips, and Kool-Aid at various booths. Be sure to have peanuts and candy at a booth manned by the camp store manager. Cotton candy and popcorn are optional.

* * *

Christmas in camp is something special. Much rainy time can be used making gifts in the craft shop. Campers can exchange names in their cabins. Cost may be limited to 10-25¢. Each gift must be made, not bought. Cabins are decorated with evergreens, cones, and soap snow. A Christmas tree is put up in the main building and campers make all their own decorations, stringing popcorn and berries to paper-chain ornaments and soapflake snow. Christmas carols are sung all day. A Christmas story can be read, told, or acted out by campers. Christmas can be celebrated rain or shine, so stockings can be hung up the night before and filled by counselors with candy, peanuts, etc. Counselors or older campers will enjoy caroling after campers are in bed and before they go to sleep. Gifts are given out around the tree on Christmas Day. A turkey dinner with trimmings adds to the occasion.

* * *

Conduct sports clinics in football, soccer, tennis, basketball, baseball, track, bowling, archery, fencing, and golf. Use counselors or staff who have competed in these sports in college or high school.

* * *

Offer a wrestling class for boys if there is a staff member who can properly instruct and supervise. One camp found it had an ex-boxer on the staff who was glad to give some pointers.

* * *

If the rifle range has a cover over the shooting area, offer this activity right through that summer shower. Conduct longer periods and include more campers in the riflery class.

* * *

Offer special activities not usually offered in good weather. One camp found a counselor who had taken karate lessons. Campers were eager to learn this new skill. Once the rain stopped the class was dropped.

* * *

Hold a cake-decorating class. Each table that night can have a cake decorated by this class.

* * *

Have a dress-up-your-counselor meal. Each cabin makes a costume from newspapers, sheets, or anything campers choose to dress their counselor. It may be a comic strip or nursery rhyme character, or guess who. At an after-dinner parade of the costumed counselors, the prettiest, most original, funniest, or most elaborate may be chosen.

* * *

How about a hobo meal? Come dressed in grubby clothes (after an all-day rain who has anything else). Eat from tin plates or washed-out soda pop cans. Food could be cooked on hobo stoves under a shelter, or served in the regular dining hall.

* * *

Try a one-utensil meal. No silverware is on the tables except serving pieces. As campers come in the dining room door, they reach into a big box for one utensil. They cannot see what they are picking up, but whatever it is, they must eat their whole meal with it. Save some special items like a soup ladle, potatomasher, and spatula for the camp leaders. Have a camera on hand for some pictures!

* * *

In a deaf and dumb meal no words may be spoken once the campers step into the dining hall. Motions are used instead of sounds. Grace is said silently and a chorus can be sung by motions only. The silence can be a welcome relief to a noisy dining hall.

* * *

Have you ever had a backward day? Start with supper and end with breakfast. Reverse the order of the day's schedule. Even the meals can begin with dessert and end with an appetizer. One camp had the campers wear their shirts backward and some wore hats with faces painted on them and walked backward into the dining hall. This will be one of the different things that campers will talk about.

* * *

Hold a talent show. Screen contestants beforehand. Put variety into the presentations (vocal, instrumental, funny, serious, stories, impersonations, etc.). Some hidden talent may be discovered.

* * *

High-schoolers profit from a careers panel. Invite some successful businessmen or professional people to be on the panel or use the camp's staff. Different vocations might even be role played. Campers frequently are not aware of the many vocational opportunities that are open.

* * *

Make tapes of camp songs for counselor training the following year. This is a good way to teach songs to new staff and campers.

* * *

Hold a lantern party in the evening. All the games, singing, and the devotional are done in lantern light. If there is a barn with hay, campers can sit in the hay for the program.

* * *

Organize a harmonica band or a comb band.

* * *

How about a cheerleading squad that practices for camp sports events?

* * *

Have a pet show. Turtles, snakes, beetles, spiders, mice, or whatever your campers can catch may be entered. Remember if they find an animal such as a chipmunk or squirrel, it should be let loose after the show or within a few days. Or, hold a pet show where each cabin enters a camper dressed as an animal. Have each animal perform; judges pick the winners.

* * *

Keep a rainy day chest of games, costumes, puzzles, and surprises. Only on the second consecutive day of rain may the chest be opened. Contents of the chest are changed from time to time. Seeing what is in the chest becomes a great event. Typical contents: candies, craft items to make, suggestions for all-day programs.

* * *

Have a Halloween party. Campers make their own costumes and come dressed as clowns, animals, or personalities. Include bobbing for apples, or eating apples hung on a string, and popping corn. Refreshments can be apple juice and doughnuts.

* * *

Hold a slave auction. Rig up a curtain so only a girl's feet are visible. Girls should be barefooted, though rings and jewelry may be worn on the toes. Fellows bid on the slaves. Slaves can be purchased for peanuts or beans. One camp used money and put it toward a camp project. Slaves who are thus bought must fan their masters, serve them meals, and wait on them for a predetermined period of time. Then the masters turn their slaves free with much ceremony.

* * *

A Noah's Ark program can seem like forty days of rain. Campers march into the camp's big building two by two and walk up a gangplank. One cabin can be birds and campers would "fly" in. Another cabin can be elephants who do an elephant walk. The lions do a trained lion act; the birds sing and each group entertains. Or play—"Guess what animal sounds like this?"

* * *

Give each camper a stick of gum to chew. When it is soft he tries to mold the gum on a file card with a toothpick. The one that looks most like an ark is the winner. Refreshments can be cow juice and animal crackers.

* * *

Hold a soap bubble-blowing contest. A variation: see who can bite the most bubbles in two minutes.

* * *

Make lots of table games available. These can be in a lounge area or used in the cabins. Invest in a few games of checkers, Clue, Monopoly, Cootie, Pick-Up-Sticks, Barrel of Monkeys, Chess, Frustration, etc.

* * *

Hold a mock TV show complete with soap opera take-off, newscast, athletic event, and a few commercials.

* * *

Walk about camp with a tape recorder and record camp sounds. Who can identify someone singing in a shower, catsup pouring from a bottle, an arrow being released from a bow, or a camp leader snoring?

* * *

Spend time getting the cabins extra clean. Hold an open house after cleanup time. Award the golden broom to the cleanest cabin and a shovel to the dirtiest.

* * *

Hold challenges in the dining hall. Who can eat the most peanut butter? Who can drink the most milk? Who does the best imitation of a chicken? A cow? A horse? Run a pie-eating contest, an egg-throwing contest with contestants moving a step away from each other after every throw. Who can do the most push-ups? Who can chin the most times on the rafters? Who can eat the most Jell-O?

* * *

Which cabin can completely cover their counselor with toilet paper first?

* * *

Form a drill team and practice for an outdoor game when the sun comes out.

* * *

Hold a marble tournament.

* * *

Bring several canoes or rowboats into the recreation hall. Have cabins decorate the boats as floats. This can be related to a theme for the week. Judge the boats for ingenuity. Provide crepe paper, chicken wire, and paint.

* * *

Hold an indoor rodeo. Use wooden horses and have races, play polo, or musical chairs on horseback. One camper on all fours can be the horse and another camper rides his back. Rig up a bucking bronco from an oil drum. Put a saddle on it and secure it with four sturdy ropes. With a camper at each rope, the bronco can be

All-Camp Activities/7

made to buck violently. See how long anyone can "ride" him. Be sure to put mattresses underneath or tie the bronc over a pile of straw.

* * *

Have a Mother Goose party for younger campers. Everyone comes dressed as a Mother Goose character. Sing nursery rhymes until nobody can think of another one.

* * *

Hold a Winnie the Pooh party. Read Pooh stories. Serve bread and honey and have red balloons because, "Nobody can be unhappy with a red balloon."

* * *

Celebrate Thanksgiving. Have a quiet time on thankfulness. Tell stories of the pilgrims. Make straw brooms in crafts or spruce-needle pillows. Learn how the early settlers lived. Climax with a turkey dinner. One camp had a roast turkey on each table and each cabin came as a family. "Father" carved the turkey and all gave thanks. The meal was complete with cranberries and pumpkin pie.

* * *

Plan candlelight vespers. Begin with a candlelight processional. A candlelight choir can sing. (Use small candles with cardboard wax shields.) Candles placed in paper bags of sand can mark the entrance to the chapel. An indoor cross with holes or brackets for candles can be constructed. As part of the processional, each camper may place his candle on the large cross until it is completely outlined in candles. This can be part of a worship or meditation service. Flickering candlelight and the sound of raindrops on the roof will help make this a long-remembered service.

* * *

On rainy days make good use of camp bulletin boards. Post riddles, quizzes, and nature exhibits for identification.

* * *

Have a progressive supper. This takes forethought and planning but it works well on a rainy day. Serve the first course of the meal in the recreation hall, the meat or main course in the dining hall, then go to the craft cabin or shelter for the beverage, and another spot for dessert. A variation of this progressive dinner is an international meal. Serve a meal of a foreign country. Have staff members dressed as nationals of that country. At each stop, while campers are eating, someone tells about its land, its people, and its climate.

* * *

Conduct a story-time through the day in the camp library. Change counselors every half hour or so.

* * *

Hold a kangaroo court, or an initiation ceremony for new campers. Bring campers to court for real or concocted offenses. Some "serious offenses": losing a shoelace, sneezing, not singing a song with a group, having blue eyes. Sentence the camper to perform some stunt. Vary the penalty. Penalties may include pushing a peanut with the nose, jumping with shoelaces tied, singing a solo, patting the head while rubbing the chest. Be careful not to humiliate anyone, but make it all fun.

* * *

Hold an Indian powwow. Use a ceremonial indoor fire, one that starts with chemicals or matches pulled across sandpaper. Have Indian games—arm wrestling, leg wrestling. Campers wear headbands of different designs, designating their cabins or tribes. Sing Indian songs such as "Land of the Silver Birch," "My Paddle Is Keen and Bright," "We Are the Red Men." (See music sources in the bibliography.)

* * *

Have a caterpillar race. All team members or all cabinmates must hold onto a rope at all times. Each group is sent to different spots around camp. At each location directions are marked where to go next. It is a race to see who finishes the course first, but the whole group must go as a caterpillar.

* * *

Trick or treat for an afternoon. Campers go begging from cabin to cabin. (Be sure to dress for rain.) At some cabins candies are given out, at others campers recieve only stones. Peanuts, popcorn, dried beans, fruit, or cookies may also be given. They get marshmallows at the last stop. These are then toasted in the fireplace. Campers make and decorate their trick-or-treat bags in the craft shop earlier.

* * *

Situation charades. Each cabin draws a slip of paper from a bag. Each paper describes a situation that cabin must act out. Here are some ideas: showing a bad report card to your father; timid camper getting into the lake for his first swimming lesson; boy at his first piano recital; child forgets his poem at a Christmas program; counselor sneaking back to his cabin after the campers are asleep.

* * *

Drama in a bag. Each cabin is given a paper bag with a dozen or so props. They must make up a skit, using all the props in the bag.

* * *

Valentine party, a dress-up affair. Decorations are red and white. Play magic heart: When the music stops, campers must touch a heart on the floor or wall. There's one less heart than campers. Someone is eliminated each time. Serve heart-shaped cookies, red Kool-Aid.

* * *

Paper bag or stocking puppet shows can be hilarious. Prepare your puppets on an afternoon of rain. Campers may write their own plays or give a fairy tale, or a story can be dramatically portrayed. The show can be given that night or the next time it rains.

* * *

Shadow plays can be fun too. Hang up a sheet and place a strong light behind it. Campers act out the scenes between the light and the sheet. Campers might try to guess the story being enacted.

* * *

The counselors can let down their hair and put on a show for the campers one afternoon or evening. One camp had the counselors imitate certain campers.

Campers were good at guessing who they were. (Be careful not to hurt feelings.) When the tables are turned, campers are quite good at taking off on their counselors' idiosyncrasies.

* * *

Who hasn't tried a camper stunt night? But it needn't be at night. Have stunts on a rainy afternoon.

* * *

Hold a clothesline art exhibit. Campers in sketching class or art classes can display their work for all of camp to enjoy.

* * *

You have probably had a camper-counselor softball game. Why not hold one indoors, using a beach ball. When running bases, the batter must put someone in a wheelbarrow and push him from base to base. The catcher must catch the ball in a bucket, butterfly net, or washtub. Use imagination for a hilarious softball game.

* * *

If the theme for the week is western, try a gold rush. Each cabin group represents prospectors searching for gold. Put a dab of yellow or gold paint on anything you want collected and campers will bring it in. One camp cleared the paths of trash this way and another removed barrels of stones from the ball field.

* * *

Learn something of the area where the campsite is located. Was it once a farm? A wilderness area? What pioneer inhabitants once lived here? What Indian tribes once roamed here? What did they live in? How did they dress? Did they make jewelry or pottery? What did it look like? Reconstruct a pioneer village in miniature or make a costume a pioneer or Indian might have worn. Have some books available for campers to find this information. Or have an old-timer come and tell campers about how it was when he was a boy in this area.

* * *

Invite a forest ranger to visit the camp and speak on conservation or land formations. Specialists in areas of nature, physical geography, or astronomy can be invited to talk to campers on rainy days.

* * *

Have a question box and plan an answer panel of staff members. Give campers an opportunity to write their questions or turn them in beforehand. A master of ceremonies can read these aloud and direct them to the panel. Older campers enjoy this kind of session.

* * *

Conduct a fire drill or an evacuation drill. This is especially good for areas that are dry, or subject to flooding.

* * *

Arrange for a field trip to a nearby museum or a planatarium, if any.

* * *

Pull off a yo-yo tournament.

* * *

Find the camper with the widest smile, loudest voice, biggest feet, lightest in weight, and the girl with the longest hair. Who can sing the highest note and who can reach the lowest? Who has the shortest name? The longest?

* * *

Nature baseball. Have on hand a collection of nature samples—leaves, rocks, wild berries, etc. The pitcher asks the batter to identify one. If he can, he goes to first base. If he can't, he's out. Three outs and the sides change.

* * *

Try a counselor hunt. At mealtime the counselors disappear one at a time. When they are all gone from the dining hall, the director can announce that bandits have captured the counselors (if the theme is western) or Captain Kidd has taken them (if the theme is about pirates) and the campers must find them. Limits should be put on time and the area where counselors hid.

* * *

Have a Sadie Hawkins Day. Fellows are given a five-minute start. Each girl tries to find and catch a boy. Eligible men counselors have bounties on their heads or are worth more in points. Set a time limit and decide on rules. If a boy climbs a tree and a girl finds him and waits at the bottom of the tree for ten minutes, he's hers. All boys caught must sit with the girls who caught them for the evening meal. He must buy her something at the canteen and she must make him a fancy hat which he must wear to the dining hall. Hats can be judged after the meal.

* * *

Go on an indoor snipe hunt. Clues can be laid in code.

* * *

Hold an indoor nature fair. Display interesting things campers have found. Discourage picking of wild flowers and, of course, do not damage trees. If a wild pet is caught, be sure to know what it eats and the kind of environment it needs before trying to keep it only a few days. Of course, you will then let it go. Have many classifications and awards, so that everyone can qualify for some recognition. Teach campers that it is better to watch than to kill. We are guardians and custodians of creation and of the delicate balance on which it survives.

* * *

Have campers put on plays. They can make costumes, scenery, and write plots. They can learn to cooperate with one another and to appreciate the contributions of others. Drama in camp can teach poise, self-discipline, good enunciation, and proper voice projection. Favorite camp songs can be included. Secular plays campers write should be funny and entertaining. The action is colorful and somewhat overacted. They should end with the audience hissing the villain or cheering the hero. The group should work closely with a counselor to avoid anything in bad taste. Involve as many campers as possible.

* * *

Reading plays is much less work. The script is read by each actor as he carries out the action.

* * *

Don't forget musical plays and contatas. John Peterson has written some excellent works which can be given by older campers and staff.

* * *

Pantomimes. Stories can be read by one person and acted out by others.

* * *

Set up a comic art museum. Some exhibits might be: one-eyed monster (needle), slipper (banana peel), diamond pin (dime and pin), something to adore (door knob), ten-carrot ring (ring made of ten carrots). Your campers will think of lots more.

* * *

With water colors, paint faces on knees. Dress up lower part of legs as clowns, ballerinas, etc. Participants stand behind a sheet with legs from knees down showing. Have them put on an act.

* * *

Rainy days should contribute to a camper's education. This is a good time to teach cooperation, teamwork, and consideration for others. Because the pace of camp is different, there will be more time for sharing, and more emphasis on right attitudes and sportsmanship. Rainy days should provide outlets for campers' creativity, ingenuity, and leadership abilities. Rainy days break up the monotony of daily routine.

3 Cabin Activities

Don't track mud in the cabin! But there are many things you *can* do as a cabin group. Make rainy days exciting days, especially if it rains at the beginning of the week, when homesickness is more likely to occur.

* * *

The fish may be biting during a warm rain and many of your campers may never have caught a fish on their very own. If there's no thunder or lightening, go fishing as a cabin.

* * *

Learn how to properly clean the fish that are caught and ask the cooks to let you cook them for supper for just your own cabin.

* * *

If campers do not have fishing equipment, why not make poles and learn fly-tying?

* * *

Make plaster casts of those deer tracks down by the lake—or maybe it was a racoon or muskrat. Can you tell which? Look it up in a book.

* * *

Set up a bird feeding station and a bird blind. Some old lumber and tarps make a good place to hide so the birds won't see you but you can see them. Place food in hanging feeders as well as ground feeders. Provide seeds, nuts, apples, and peanut butter. Mark different locations with numbered markers so you can call the attention of your cabinmates to a bird at #4 station. Leave some small brush for cover. Rope off the area so campers do not walk through the feeder area and scare away the birds. Campers will have hours of fun watching different birds feeding and will attract more birds than they knew were around.

* * *

From an old tarp or piece of canvas make a toilet article case for each of the campers. It might look like this:

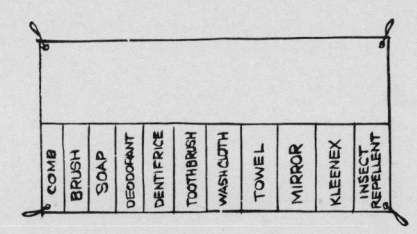

| COMB | BRUSH | SOAP | DEODORANT | DENTIFRICE | TOOTHBRUSH | WASHCLOTH | TOWEL | MIRROR | KLEENEX | INSECT REPELLENT |

It can be hung across the bottom of a bed (don't keep wet washcloths and towels in it) or folded in half lengthwise, rolled up, and tied for trips.

* * *

Follow an onion trail. Have someone go ahead and rub a cut onion on leaves and bushes, then try to follow the trail by smelling the onion as you go. Don't forget the rainwear.

* * *

Compose and illustrate Japanese Haiku. This is an unrhymed poem of three lines containing five, seven, and five syllables respectively. It usually refers in some way to the seasons of the year. You might begin by reading Haiku. Close your eyes and see a mental picture.

    I stand on the hill
    As the wind blows against me,
    I see the storm come.

Compose some of these about the out-of-doors around the camp.

* * *

As a cabin, put on a midget show for another cabin or for the rest of camp. One camper puts socks and shoes on his hands and puts his arms under the first camper's armpits. The illusion is of a funny little dwarf. You can have him feed himself, shave himself (remove the blade from the razor), or wash his face, which is all done by the person behind who cannot see what he is doing.

* * *

Or you may bring storybook characters to life. On poster board cut out head and arm holes. Paint bodies on the poster board. Pieces of material may also be glued on.

* * *

Similar to this is composite art on folded paper. Here the first person draws the head, folding his drawing over so the next artist can't see the head. Others draw the neck, chest, and so on. In each instance drawings are folded over so no one will know what the end result looks like. The last person puts a name on it. When the folded paper is opened, roars of laughter follow.

* * *

Young campers enjoy listening to stories, either told by counselors or by a recording.

* * *

If a counselor is good at telling stories, ask campers to make a list of things they want in a story (horse, broken chair, kite, etc.). The storyteller weaves into his plot all of the objects on the campers' list. At one camp this was a regular weekly event, a continued story. Campers sometimes stayed another week just to hear the next episode told by an excellent storyteller. If the rain continues, so can the story.

* * *

Make weather flags for the boating area.

* * *

Waterproof matches with parafin or make trench candles. Cut newspaper strips about 3''-5'' wide. Wrap tightly until as thick as your thumb. Tie with string and leave a foot or so of extra string. Drop into melted parafin. When saturated, hang up to dry. Use them to start fires in wet weather.

* * *

Have campers illustrate a book they have read. Others guess what book it is.

* * *

Make place mats for the dining hall. Leaves, ferns, and grasses may be pressed between two pieces of wax paper with a cool iron. Edges may be scalloped or cut with pinking shears.

* * *

Wall hangings made of two pieces of colored plastic film may be used to seal in prepressed leaves and ferns. Seal top, bottom, and sides with tape. These may be used to decorate the chapel or cabins.

* * *

Run a turtle race. Draw a circle, place turtles in the center. The first one to get out of the circle wins.

* * *

Play truth or consequences. Make up foolish questions: On what date is the 4th of July celebrated? And impossible questions: How many gallons of water are in our lake? Consequences should be funny for everyone.

* * *

Hold a debate on some subject of interest or some nonsense topic. Resolved: Cats are more intelligent than dogs.

* * *

Try analyzing handwriting of the camp staff.

* * *

Exchange riddles with cabinmates.

* * *

Practice physical fitness skills.

* * *

Hold a slimnastics class in your cabin.

* * *

The campers may enjoy playing indoor games: charades, 20 questions, rhythm or animal rhythm, mental games, magic games.

* * *

Maybe this would be a good time to wash clothes, sew on those missing buttons, or repair that bursting seam.

* * *

A rainy day is just right for digging for fishing worms.

* * *

Exchange experiences: my most embarrassing moment, my happiest experience, the funniest thing that ever happened to me.

* * *

Have a "tea" for girls.

* * *

Write folk songs or poetry.

* * *

Conduct a first aid class. The new American Red Cross Multimedia System standard course can be taught in eight hours, or two four-hour blocks. This is great for a rainy day, but advance planning is necessary to secure the free films from Red Cross and have a qualified instructor to teach. Encourage someone on the staff to take the necessary training prior to camp.

* * *

Girls will enjoy trying different hair styles and fixing each other's hair, or conducting a good grooming class.

* * *

Decide on a shield, motto, and color for the cabin this

week. Make cabin pins from toothpicks and alphabet noodles or wood-burn the cabin motto on small pins made from cross sections of branches. Make medallions with the motto or shield on them. Wear the cabin colors. Make a larger shield for the cabin door from a cross section of a log.

* * *

Make funny hats from newspaper or construction paper to wear to the dining hall.

* * *

Include a marshmallow roast for your cabin, or toast s'mores around a fireplace.

* * *

Put together a camp newspaper. Some campers can type; others can do layout. Some can write news items. You can include a gossip column, comic strip, and editorial. Some campers can be reporters and interview various staff members about their goals, hobbies, and their experiences. Older campers can cut stencils and your camp newspaper can be mimeographed. A counselor with experience or a journalism student could sponsor the newspaper.

* * *

Have a nature hunt with cabinmates. Find something that crawls, a seed, prickly leaf, compound leaf, square stem, parasite, etc. Send campers out for one thing at a time. See who can find each item first and who finds the most.

* * *

Make utensils for your next camp-out. Try making fire tongs, pot hooks, or slides for adjusting tent ropes or weave a green stick broiler.

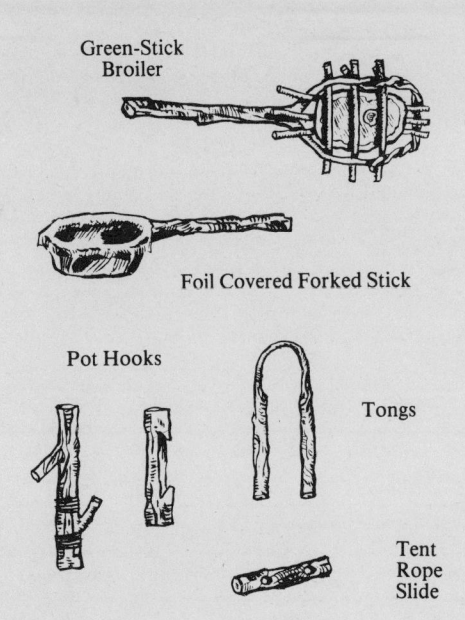

* * *

Green-Stick Broiler

Foil Covered Forked Stick

Pot Hooks

Tongs

Tent Rope Slide

Or make equipment from tin cans.

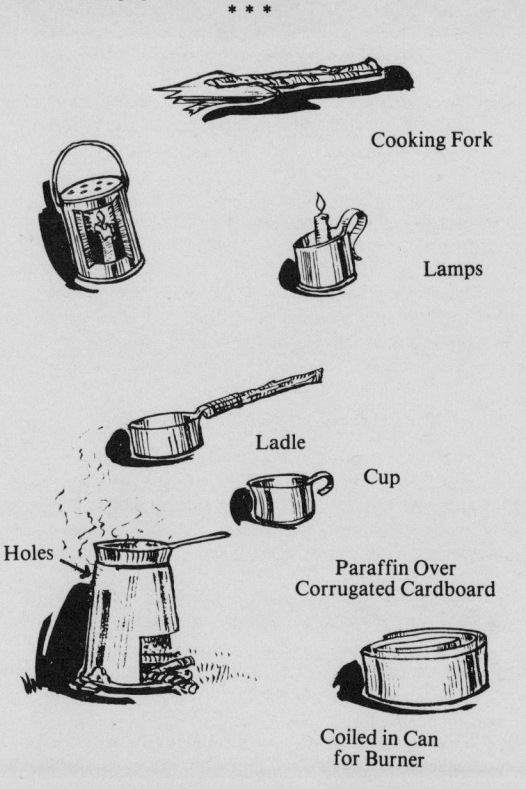

* * *

Cooking Fork

Lamps

Ladle

Cup

Holes

Paraffin Over Corrugated Cardboard

Coiled in Can for Burner

Start an insect zoo. Crickets, praying mantises, or walking sticks can be placed in fancy cages campers make. Collect food for the zoo animals. A good way to do this is to shake a bush and collect tiny insects on a sheet or umbrella. Find out what the zoo inmates eat and give them the right diet.

* * *

Start a seed collection.

* * *

Juniors are great collectors. A rainy day is a good day to begin a rock collection, twig or bark collection, leaf or wood collection, or feather collection.

* * *

Play paper and pencil games in the cabin. Do crossword puzzles or find hidden names in scrambled letters.

* * *

Start a desert garden or terrarium. Go for a rain walk and collect mosses and ground pine.

* * *

Collect tadpoles. Put them in an aquarium and watch them grow. Add rock or land areas for when they emerge as frogs.

* * *

Draw a large bird on poster board. Paste all the feathers that campers can find around camp on the bird. This will give campers an idea of the great variety of interesting birds in the area. Try to cover the paper bird with feathers.

* * *

Role-play situations that teens may face when they go home. This might include dealing with problems. Campers will gain valuable insights and be better prepared to carry over lessons they have learned in camp.

* * *

Make a 3-D layout of the campsite. Use a sand table or make a permanent layout with flour, water, and salt. Place all the buildings on the display in the proper places. Use pine cones for trees or small pieces of sponge painted green. Use blue cardboard or a mirror for the lake or pool.

* * *

Plan a party with another cabin.

* * *

Bake a cake in a fireplace and ice it with melted chocolate bars and marshmallows.

* * *

Have a taffy pull. Or make pizza or fudge.

* * *

Conduct a fashion show or a class in etiquette. Using a skit method can make this interesting as well as informative.

* * *

Start a barbershop quartet.

* * *

Appoint a scribe for the cabin and keep a log of cabin activities. Include all the funny things that happen. Send copies to campers after they return home.

* * *

Plan a backpacking trip. Choose committees of wood-gatherers, fire builders, cooks, KPs, programmers. Decide the menus with the cabin (be sure they are balanced). Decide how to prepare the food: Will you fry, broil, bake, boil, toast, roast, stew, or poach? Use a map to decide where to go, and what trails to follow. Estimate where you will spend each night and what you will do along the way. Check the mileage. Write a trip plan with distances to landmarks. Note any steep climbs by checking the contour lines on your map. Discuss clothing and give each camper a checklist of things to take. Decide on a theme for the trip and plan evening programs to follow that theme. Include games, songs, and stunts. Change the names of food items and games to fit the theme. (Hamburger, carrots, and potatoes can be jungle stew for a safari trip. A game of "steal the bacon" may become "rustling the cattle" for a western theme.) Give instructions on how to pack gear, keeping the weight high and close to the body. Review how to set up your shelters and first aid. All preparations can be made while the rain is still falling; the trip can start on the first clear day.

* * *

A canoe trip can also be planned on a rainy day. Pack gear in waterproof boxes that can be easily carried through a portage. Check map for rapids, waterfalls, and portages. Plot overnight spots and likely rest stops.

* * *

Make a fire board of miniature fire lays. Make a knot board, displaying the many knots used in camp. A display board of ways to pitch a tarp can be made with small sticks and little squares of cloth. These instructional tools can be used in teaching campcraft.

* * *

Keep on hand for that rainy day some service projects for a nearby hospital, or convalescent home, or home for the aged. Write to them before camp and ask for a list of things campers could do or make for them.

* * *

Polish all shoes in the cabin and waterproof the hiking boots.

* * *

Start a progressive story, have each camper add to it.

* * *

Make some cabin games. Paint tick-tack-toe, checkers, or shuffleboard on the cabin floor. Make checkers from slices of a tree branch. Shuffleboard equipment can be made from forked sticks and wood circles.

* * *

Make a ring-toss game or bean bag game and contribute it to the camp's game supply. Make and carve hiking sticks. Make a toss-and-catch game, or stilts.

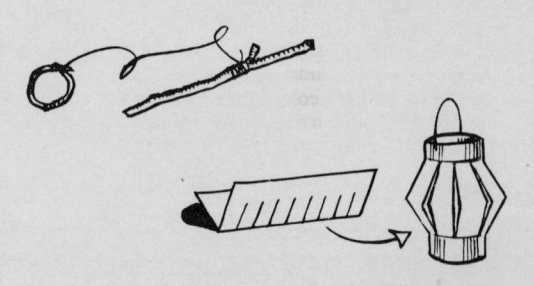

* * *

Make Japanese lanterns to decorate the cabin or recreation hall.

* * *

Make flags of other nations and display them in the dining hall.

* * *

Make party favors or place markers for the banquet using birchbark, paper, shells, wood, bark, driftwood, or ferns.

* * *

If you can get the materials, try making a tent for the cabin's use. The *Golden Book of Camping* and *Camp Crafts* have instructions for making tents and camping equipment.

* * *

Make a ditty bag for next week's hike. Several campers can work together to make a tarp or backpack.

* * *

Construct a planetarium. Draw the skyline around a particular spot on your campsite. Lightly draw in the star locations from a star map or chart. Then on a clear night, check the planetarium for accuracy before finishing it.

* * *

Learn types of lashing and uses of each—square, diagonal, sheer, continuous. Dressed in ponchos, collect wood to construct some useful piece of furniture. Bring the wood indoors and make a bench, table, chair, porch swing, or night stand for your cabin.

* * *

Study an area of soil erosion on the campsite. Make plans as a cabin group to correct it. This may mean log steps on a steep trail to hold back the soil, or planting proper ground covers on a bare area. Campers may decide to move the location of a trail, or put rocks in a gully to hold the soil.

* * *

Make a weather station and give daily weather reports to the whole camp. See bibliography for sources.

* * *

Using plaster of Paris or clay over wire forms, make replicas of snakes found in the area. These should be accurate in size and color when painted. They can be used for identification and can be helpful to the camp if it is located in snake country.

* * *

A drippy, soggy day is good for a rap session in the cabin. Older campers especially enjoy this.

* * *

Have a camp improvement afternoon. Fix bulletin boards; repair and paint camp benches; repair song books; decorate dining hall and cabins; repair leaks.

* * *

Make posters for safety, fire prevention, or the camp's conservation program.

* * *

An older cabin group may prepare an evening program for younger campers.

* * *

Prepare a worship service for the whole camp led by your cabin.

* * *

Practice using a knife, ax, and saw. Whittle something, chop firewood, saw some logs to keep the fires going all day in the lodge so other campers can come in and get dry.

* * *

Play tournaments—round robin ping-pong, shuffleboard, ten pins, box hockey, skittles.

* * *

Make star maps of the various constellations. This can be done with gummed stars on blue constuction paper or pin-pricked holes in cardbaord with a flashlight held behind it. Old black 35mm slides can be pinholed and projected on a screen.

* * *

Make an electrical quiz board for a Nature Nook. Or set up a "What's it?" box or peep boxes.

* * *

Have a cookout in a fireplace. Plan a special meal with food not usually available in the dining hall. Campers can make upside-down cake or cherry cobbler in an iron pot.

* * *

If you have tried a half dozen of these ideas, the rain has probably stopped, so dry out your bedding, hang up the wet jeans and socks, and bask in the sunshine!

4 Individual Activities

When the clouds are leaking and washcloths are mildewing, better plan some sharp activities for campers to do individually. Johnny may want to write letters, but Steve is raring to collect salamanders. Jane would rather get her clothes mended, but Pat would rather read poetry. Rainy days are good days to consider the individual differences of campers and provide lots of things they can do on their own, as well as cabin and whole-camp activities.

* * *

Open the camp library and make good use of the library bulletin board to display book jackets and promote some of the newer books. Some campers can work in the library and repair or catalog books.

* * *

Collect rock specimens and display them in an egg carton after they are identified.

* * *

Collect spiderwebs in the rain. These can be caught on a piece of construction paper or cardboard. The web can be sprayed with silver paint first, then collected on a dark-colored paper. Use a piece larger than the web; bring the paper from behind the web carefully so as not to disturb the pattern.

* * *

Rainy days are good for arts and crafts. Be sure to have extra staff available to help in the craft shop on those damp days. Some items must be completed in the shop, while others, such as lanyards and bracelets can be finished in front of the fireplace or in the cabin. Here are some craft ideas:

—Shellcraft. Jewelry, pins, necklaces, bracelets, earrings, cuff links, and shell-covered boxes can be made or decorated with small colored shells. Larger shells can be used for small lamps or mottoes. Animals made from shells are popular with campers.

—Block printing can be used to decorate stationery, place mats, T-shirts, scarves, etc. Cut a design from a linoleum block, potato, eraser, or a stick. Ferns or leaves make good prints, too.

—Stenciling. Make pennants, flags, or mark backpack equipment.

—Fabric decorating. Make vests, curtains for your cabin, scarves, etc., by putting designs on your own fabrics. This can be done by block printing, screen printing, applique, tube painting, bleaching, embroidering, spatter painting, or tie-dying.

—Braiding and knotting. Macrame belts, vests, scarves, headbands, handbags, lanyards, bolo ties, earrings, rings, pins, and corsages can be made with knotting and braiding. Jute cord, leather, string, or craft strip can be used. Bracelets can be braided or wrapped over a cardboard or metal frame and wrapped with flat weave, twisted or overbraided. Try rope making or a hammock.

—Nature prints from leaves, ferns, and mushrooms make interesting prints on stationery or place mats.

—Pressed flowers, leaves, and grasses between wax paper and Kleenex tissues can make decorative place cards, mats, stationery, or bookmarks.

—Seeds from watermelon, oranges, or cantaloupe can be dried, painted, and strung for jewelry—or glued on a cardboard background and painted for mosaics or scenry pictures.

—Mobiles can be made from cones, pods, glass pieces, folded paper, shells, driftwood, wire, cans, or just about anything that isn't nailed down.

—Sawdust sculpture. To do your own thing in sculpturing, use 2 cups of sawdust to 1 cup wallpaper paste and 1/4 cup of plaster of Paris and enough water to soften the mixture.

—String weaving. Use nails to outline a picture or to fasten strings and you'll come up with some interesting geometric drawings. Use different colors of string for variety.

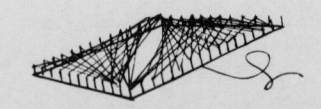

—Have an overabundance of one kind of breakfast cereal? Make cereal pictures.

—Paper mosaics. Tear up colored construction paper into small pieces. Draw a picture or design and fill in the color with pasted pieces of colored paper.

—Make a stained glass window for the camp chapel with crayoned paper or colored tissue paper. Use salad oil to make the pictures transparent.

—Make a kite to fly on a clear day.

—Young campers enjoy string prints or designs. Holding one end of a 12-inch piece of string, dip the string into paint. Squeeze some of the paint off and drag the string over the paper until you have a pleasing design. Do this with several strings in different colors of paint.

—Sponge prints. Dip pieces of sponge into paint and decorate murals, wallhangings, T-shirts, jeans, place mats, etc.

—Make a diorama of a frontier village, or make a diorama of the campsite.

—Ceramics. Some equipment will be needed for this craft, but the dividends are great if the cost can be put into budget. You'll need a kiln (it is difficult to maintain the temperature over a wood fire), clay, glazes, stilts, and guide sticks. You may be fortunate enough to have natural clay on your camp property. Clay may be molded free form, pressed into molds, or poured into molds, or coil or slab methods can be used. Decorating can be done by glazing, incising, embossing, slip painting, or graffito.

—If you are fortunate enough to have birch on your property and if you have a tree downed by the wind or storm, you will have some beautiful logs with which to make candle holders, bookends, plaques, etc. The bark can be used to make many things, from drinking cups to post cards. But *never* take bark from a living tree.

—Wood can be chip-carved, woodburned with an electric needle, painted, whittled, stained, carved, or decorated with decals. Items made from wood on the campsite are too numerous to mention, but here are a few: whistles, bookends, tie racks, napkin holders, pins, buttons, plaques, boxes, tent pegs, name tags, toggles, letter racks, buckles, games, frames for pictures, salt/pepper shakers, book covers, initials, stools, candle holders, cutting boards.

—Grow a crystal garden. Place pieces of brick or coal the size of walnuts in a dish. Add 4 tbps. salt (not iodized), 4 tbs. vinegar, 1 tb. ammonia, and 4 tbs. of liquid bluing or food dyes, and watch the garden grow.

—Pine cone zoo. Birds and animals can be made from pine cones, toothpicks, glue, and seeds.

—Fabric dyeing and tie-dyeing. Dyes can be purchased, but preferably make your own dyes from plants and berries growing on the campgrounds. For a blue color use blackberries, sunflower seeds, or larkspur flowers. For red use beets, inner bark of cedar, hemlock bark, rotten roots of a sycamore, raspberries, or dandelion roots. For yellow use sassafras bark, sumac roots, thistle flowers, elderberry leaves, bayberry leaves. For green use laurel leaves or spinach. For brown use black walnut shells, red oak bark, or hickory bark. Use about a peck of natural materials for a pound of cloth to be dyed. Prepare the same as bought dyes. Try tie-dying: tie material in a series of knots. Each knot can be dyed a different color or the whole article can be dyed one color. It will come out with sunburst patterns of color and places where the material was tied tightly will be left the original color. Clothing, curtains, and wall hangings can be decorated this way.

—Wirecraft. Bending copper, silver, or gold-colored wire can make lovely jewelry items.

—Metal. Sconces can be made from tin cans. Copper sheeting can be tooled, stippled, etched, embossed, and antiqued. Dishes, bowls, and jewelry can be made from copper or aluminum sheeting.

—Leathercraft. Projects include bags, purses, moccasins, wallets, belts, watchbands, book covers, quivers for arrows, lanyards, knife sheaths, boots, and coasters. Leather may be braided, dyed, tooled, painted, stamped, carved, fringed, beaded, and burned with an electric needle.

—Nature pictures may be made from milkweed, pods, and seeds glued to cardboard or wood. These may be sprayed with paint or gilted. Sand can be dyed and used to make pictures by filling in areas with different colors of sand. Some interesting almost three-dimensional pictures may be made with mosses, bark, and a little paint or plaster. Campers can make creative displays and take a bit of camp home with them.

—Basketry. This is an old craft. Mats, coasters, and wastebaskets can be made from grasses, raffia, or reeds.

—Make a willow whistle, a tom-tom from a tin can and inner tubes, or rattles from gourds.

—Weaving. Make a homemade loom from a wooden box. Weave mats, or sit-upons to sit on at campfire.

16/Raindrops Keep Falling on My Tent

Weave jersey loops or make mats of grasses or pine needles.

—Soap-carving. Using large cakes of Ivory soap can give a camper his first taste of carving. And if he ruins it, the soap need not be wasted.

—Glass bottles can be cut and made into useful vases and candle holders.

—Decoupage is the art of transferring pictures to another surface. Reproductions of great art can be put on wooden articles and made to look like expensive antiques.

—Foil leaf art gives a metallic finish to craft articles by the process of gluing metal leaft to articles.

—Cork can be used to decorate wood, metal, or plastic. Toys, coasters, bulletin boards can be painted, burned, or decorated with sequins and wood.

—Clay modeling. A good downpour should give campers lots of mud. Have them try modeling some of it. Figurines, tiles, and bowls can be made with the right consistency.

—Crewel work. With yarn and burlap, campers can make vests, pillows, pictures, and handbags.

—Stained glass. From broken glass, mobiles, window hangings, lamp shades, and jewerly can be made by using metal channels or a glass seal. Glass may be fitted into trays and sealed with grout or papier-mache.

—Felt flowers, slippers, pillows, hats, belts, birds, purses can be made from scraps. Felt may be emroidered, braided, painted, sewed, appliqued, and glued.

—Papier-mache bowls, pitchers, dishes, jewelry, vases, and animals can be easily made by creative campers. You can buy papier-mache mix or make your own from old newspapers and wallpaper paste.

—Cracked marbles are made by heating marbles in an oven and plunging them into cold water. Jewelry, key chains, and centerpieces can be made from these.

—Make dioramas in egg shells. Older campers may enjoy making these as place cards for the camp banquet.

—Make stone animals or figures. Paint smooth, round stones. Glue stones together with a strong glue. Pieces of felt or cloth may be used to dress your figures.

—Jelly bean animals are fun to make—and to eat.

—So are marshmallow snowmen.

—Try sandcasting. Pour plaster of Paris into sand mold. Add pebbles, glass, beads, or buttons. Add a hairpin for a hanger.

—Make paper beads. Roll small wedges of colored paper. Paint or shellac and string your beads.

—Do wax sculptures. Melt old candles. Carve with orange sticks or knives. Paint with acrylics.

—Make snowflake paperweights. Use jars with screw lids. Glue small plastic figurines to the inside of lid. Fill jar to the rim with water. Add two tsps. of moth flakes, screw on lid, and glue.

—Make Indian costumes from felt or leather.

—Make large tissue paper flowers to decorate a cabin or camp's chapel.

—Make a collage. Paste a large assortment of materials to a background. Things gathered from outdoors make lovely collections for a collage. Vary sizes, colors, and textures. Cover a whole wall with nature collages.

—Make wind chimes from tin can lids or shells. Hang these on the cabin porch. They can be painted or decorated with yarn.

—Try plastic casting. Embed nuts, insects, flowers, and leaves in solid plastic for paperweights or key ring fobs.

—Newsprint and the charcoal remains of a fire can be all you need for a charcoal sketch. Draw what you see through one small window pane. This will frame the picture.

Copper enameling. You will need a copper kiln, copper blanks, powdered glass in various colors, and possibly threads and lumps of glass. Bracelets, pins, cuff links, tie tacks, rings, medallions, necklaces, and belts can be made by enameling, overlay, graffito, and swirling. Larger pieces, for small trays, dishes, and coasters, can be worked on by older campers.

—Candle-making. Wax can be poured into molds, or into damp sand. Sequins, glitter, or whipped wax can be used to decorate candles. Candles may be painted or the wax can be colored with old crayons. Wax poured into a milk carton of ice will have a lacy appearance when hardened.

—Practice origami (paper folding). Make coasters, designs, or paper figures by folding paper.

—Young campers might enjoy making finger puppets of storybook characters and telling the stories to each other in the cabin.

—Learn knots and splices. Demonstrate eye splice, long and short splicing.

—Draw a series of sketches or impressionistic art: how

I feel when I am lonely; how I feel when I am happy; how I feel on a sunny day.

—Do laundry—if you have a dryer handy.

* * *

By the time you have tried five percent of these ideas, take a look out the window. Probably the sun will be shining. Maybe some camper will say, "Aw, there's the sun—I want to stay at camp until it rains again."

SOURCES

Tandy Leather Co., 1001 Foch St., Ft. Worth, TX 76107

American Handicrafts, 1001 Foch St., Ft. Worth, TX 76107

Economy Handicrafts, Little Neck, NY 11363

Creative Hands, P.O. Box 11602, Pittsburgh, PA 15228

World Wide Games, Inc., Box 450, Delaware, OH 43015

Educational Activities, P.O. Box 392, Freeport, NY 11520

Magnus Craft Materials, 108 Franklin St., New York, NY 10013

Forest Service, U.S. Department of Agriculture, Washington, D.C. 20250

National Audubon Society, Audubon House, 1130 Fifth Ave., New York, NY 11028

National Wildlife Federation, 1412 Sixteenth St. NW, Washington, D.C. 10036

Plymouth Cordage Co. (Knots and Ropes), Plymouth, MA 02363

Silva Co., (Compasses, Orienteering), LaPorte, IN 46350

American Camping Association, Bradford Woods, Martinsville, IN 46151

Christian Camping International, Box 400, Somonauk, IL 60552

Moody Institute of Science, 12000 E. Washington Blvd., Whittier, CA 90606

American Red Cross, 17 and D Streets N.W., Washington, D.C. 20006

BIBLIOGRAPHY

ARTS AND CRAFTS

Basketry, Boy Scouts, New Brunswick, N.J.
Knots and How to Tie Them, Boy Scouts, New Brunswick, N.J.
The Complete Book of Pottery Making, John B. Kenny, Chilton
Creative Crafts for Campers, Catherine T. Hammett and Carol Horrocks, Association Press
Easy Crafts for Juniors, Carolyn Howard, Zondervan
Easy Crafts, Ellsworth Jaeger, Macmillan
Handicraft, Lester Griswold, American Camping Association
Indian and Camp Handicraft, W. Ben Hunt, Bruce
Pack-O-Fun Series, Clapper
Learning About Nature Through Crafts, Virginia Musselman, Stackpole

NATURE

Collect, Print and Paint from Nature, John Hawkinson, American Camping Association
Creative Nature Crafts, R. O. Bale, Burgess
The Golden Nature Guide Series, *Birds, Butterflies and Moths, Fishes, Flowers, Fossils, Game Birds, Insects, Mammals, Non-Flowering Plants, Reptiles, and Amphibians, Rocks and Minerals, Seashores, Seashells of the World, Stars, Trees, Weather,* and *Zoology*, Golden Press
A Field Guide to Birds, Roger Tory Peterson, Houghton-Mifflin (In this same series are field guides to shells, butterflies, mammals, animal tracks, and ferns)
Learning About Nature Through Games, Virginia Musselman, Stackpole
The Nature Program at Camp, Janet Nickelsburg, Burgess
Look What I Found, Marshall Case, Chatham Press
Acclimatization, Steve Van Matre, American Camping Association
Acclimatizing, Steve Van Matre, American Camping Association
How to Attract, House and Feed Birds, Walter E. Schutz, Collier
OBIS-ACA Camp Kit 2, American Camping Association

CAMPCRAFT

Home in Your Pack, Bradford Angier, Stackpole
Finding Your Way in the Outdoors, Robert L. Mooers, Jr., E. P. Dutton & Co.
Be an Expert with Map and Compass, Bjorn Kjellstrom, American Orienteering Service, N.Y.
Your Own Book of Campcraft, Catherine Hammett, Simon & Schuster
Complete Book of Outdoor Lore, Clyde Ormand, Outdoor Life
Campers' Guide to Woodcraft and Outdoor Life, Luis M. Henderson, Dover
Outdoor Survival Skills, Larry Dean Olsen, Brigham Young University
The Wilderness Route Finder, Calvin Rutstrum, Macmillan
Roughing It Easy, Dian Thomas, Brigham Young University

PROGRAM

Camping Together as Christians, John and Ruth Ensign, John Knox Press
Camping for Christian Youth, Pauline and Floyd Todd, Baker
Archery, Boy Scouts, New Brunswick, N.J.
The Camp Program Book, Catherine Hammett and Virginia Musselman, Association Press
Handbook of Indian Games and Stunts, Darwin A. Hindman, Prentice-Hall
Picture-Taking in Camp, Eastman Kodak, Rochester, N.Y.
Fun with Skits, Stunts, and Stories, Helen and Larry Eisenberg, Association Press
Inspirational Poetry for Camp and Youth Groups, H. Jean Berger, Burgess
Camp Counseling, Mitchell, Crawford and Roberson
The Handbook of Skits and Stunts, Helen and Larry Eisenberg, Association Press
Program Activities for Camp, H. Jean Berger, Burgess
My Keys to Creative Ceremonies, Myra Nagel, Moore and Moore

GAMES

Fun Encyclopedia, E. O. Harbin, Abingdon
Omnibus of Fun, Helen and Larry Eisenberg, Association Press
The Cokesbury Game Book, Arthur M. Depew, Abingdon
Handy Games, Cooperative Recreation, Delaware, Ohio
Complete Book of Campfire Programs, LaRue A. Thurston, Association Press
Learning About Nature Through Games, Virginia Musselman, Stackpole

MUSIC

Anywhere Songs, Inter-Varsity Press
Tent and Trail Songs, Cooperative Recreation, Delaware, Ohio
Sing, American Camping Association
Boy Scout Song Book, Boy Scouts of America, New Brunswick, N.J.
The Ditty Bag, Janet Tobitt, Girl Scouts
ABC's of Camp Music, Janet Tobitt, American Camping Association

My Soapbox, Folk Songs, Zondervan

* * *

Write to American Camping Association, Bradford Woods, Martinsville, IN 46151 for a catalog of books and materials in these categories which are currently available.

Acknowledgments

To Awana Camps for permission to publish some of their program ideas, and to Word of Life Camps, where many of these ideas have made for successful programming on rainy days.